Sunshine comes from an enormous star in our galaxy called the Sun. The Sun's light and heat take about 8 minutes to reach us here on Earth.

the Sun

the Moon

Earth

Earth is one of 8 planets that orbit (go around) the Sun. The further a planet is from the Sun, the colder it is there. Earth is the third planet from the Sun.

Our sun started off as a massive cloud of dust and gas. Very, very slowly, the cloud formed a ball, which got hotter and hotter until it became the Sun.

a gas cloud

The Sun is mainly made up of two sorts of gases. We use one of those gases in balloons to make them float.

The other gas is burned inside the Sun. This makes the Sun extremely hot. The core (the middle) of the Sun is its hottest part. The outer layer is much cooler, but it is still so hot that it could boil rocks!

The Sun is the reason we have day and night.

As our planet orbits the Sun, it spins around. When the side of the planet we are on is opposite the Sun, we can see its light and feel its heat. We call this daytime.

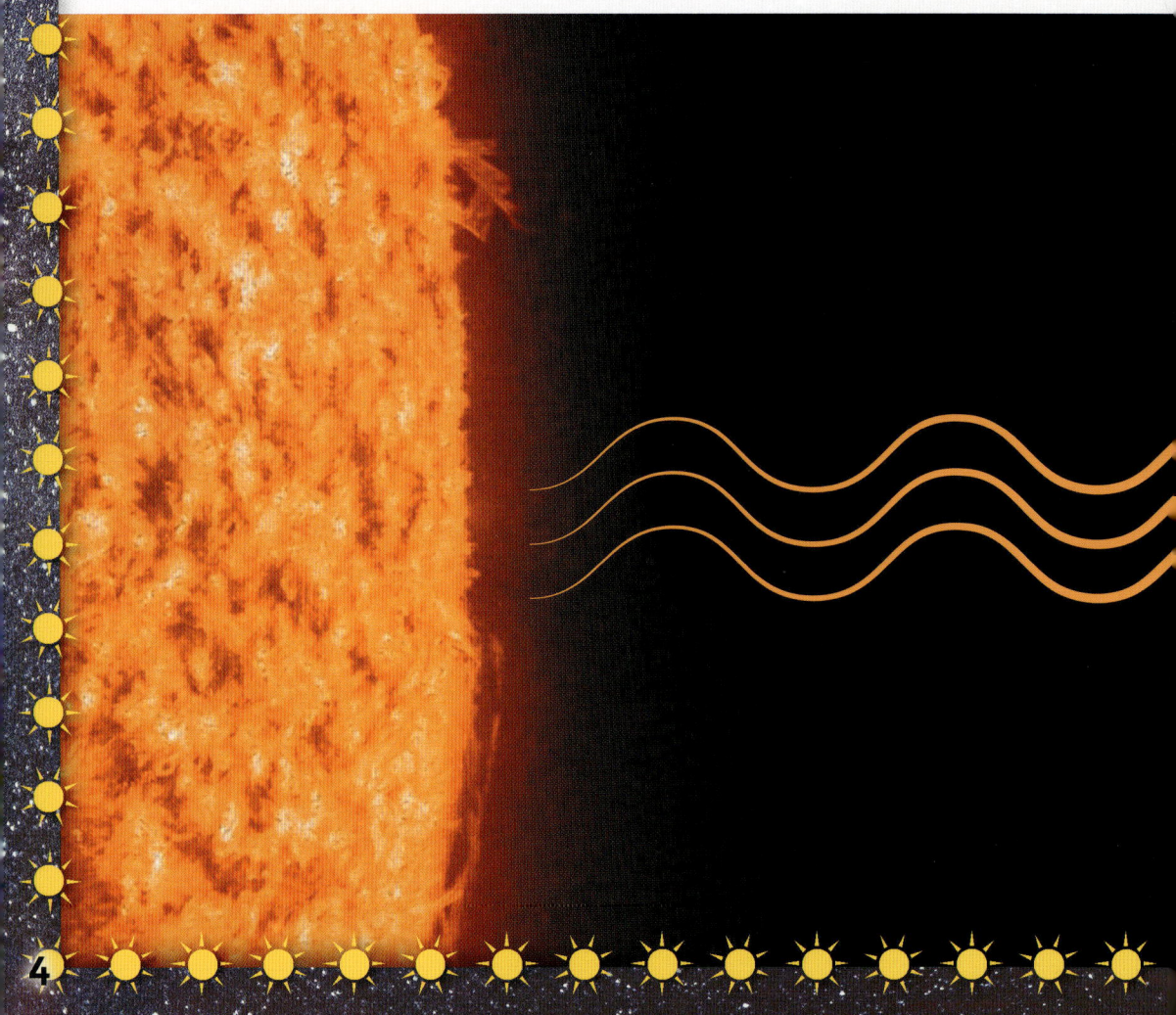

At nighttime we cannot see the Sun, but it never goes away. Instead, our planet spins around so that the other side of the Earth is opposite the Sun. This means that when it is daytime in Africa it will be nighttime in New Zealand, and the other way around.

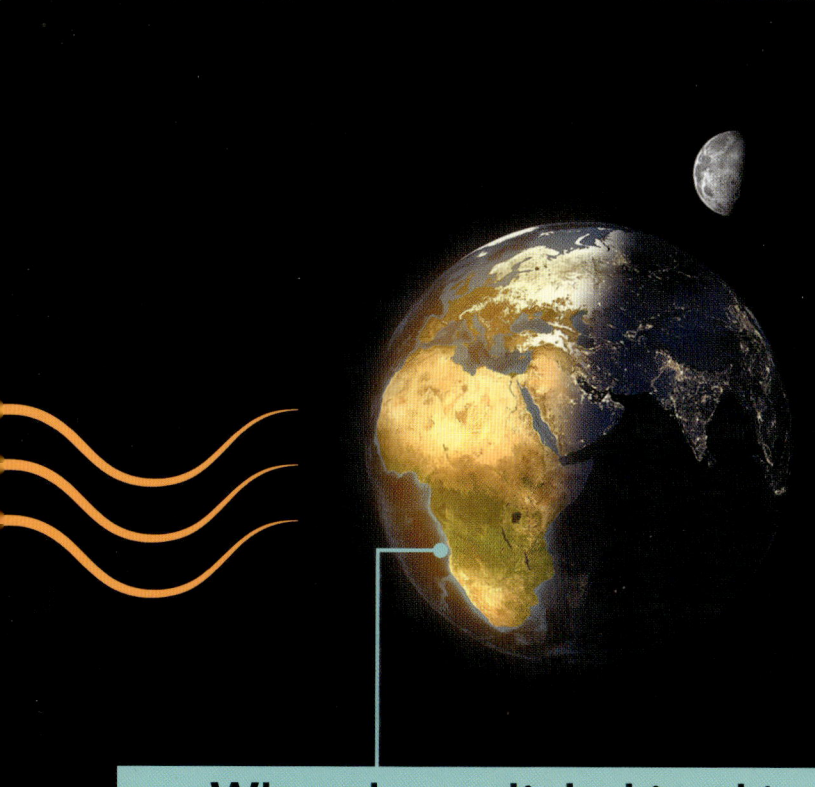

When the sunlight hits this side of the Earth, the other side is in darkness.

Did you know that sunlight feeds trees? Trees and flowers absorb (take in) the sunlight into their leaves, and then turn it into food.

Trees and flowers are at the bottom of the food chain. This means that nearly every living thing eats them, or eats something that eats them. Because the trees and flowers feed on sunlight, this means that there might not be any life on Earth at all without the Sun.

# The Food Chain

The Sun

The trees' leaves absorb the sunlight.

Leaves

Herbivores

Herbivores, like this springbok, eat the leaves.

Carnivores

Carnivores, like this cheetah, eat the herbivores and other animals.

It is not just leaves that absorb sunlight. We absorb it into our skin. We use it to make vitamin D, which is important for strong, healthy bones.

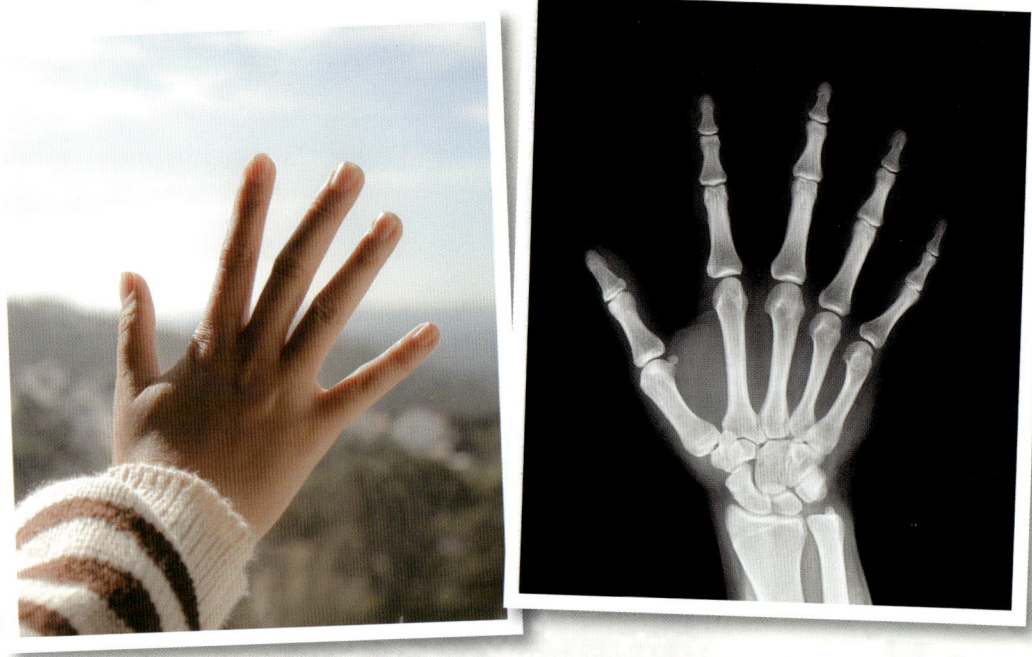

However, too much sunlight can be very bad for your skin.

If you are out in strong sunlight for a long time, you can get sunburn, which is quite painful.

# How to stay safe in the sun

1. Stay in the shade in the hottest part of the day.

2. Put on a long-sleeved top or shirt.

3. Rub some sun cream onto your skin.

4. Put on some shades to protect your eyes (/iez/).

5. Put on a wide-brimmed sun hat.

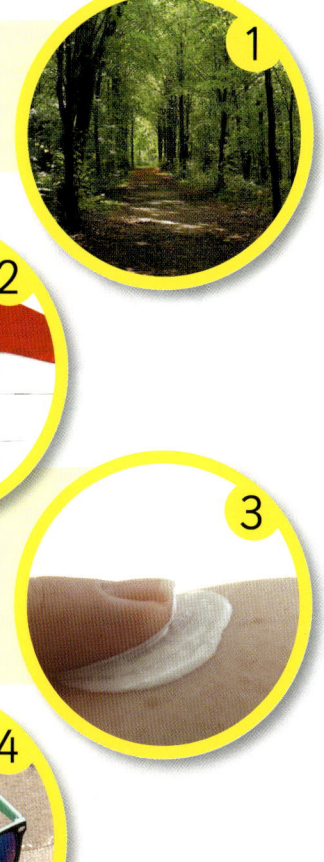

Did you know that the Sun has spots?

They are not like the spots that we get on our skin, but instead are darker patches on the outer layer of the Sun. They look darker because they are cooler than the rest of the Sun.

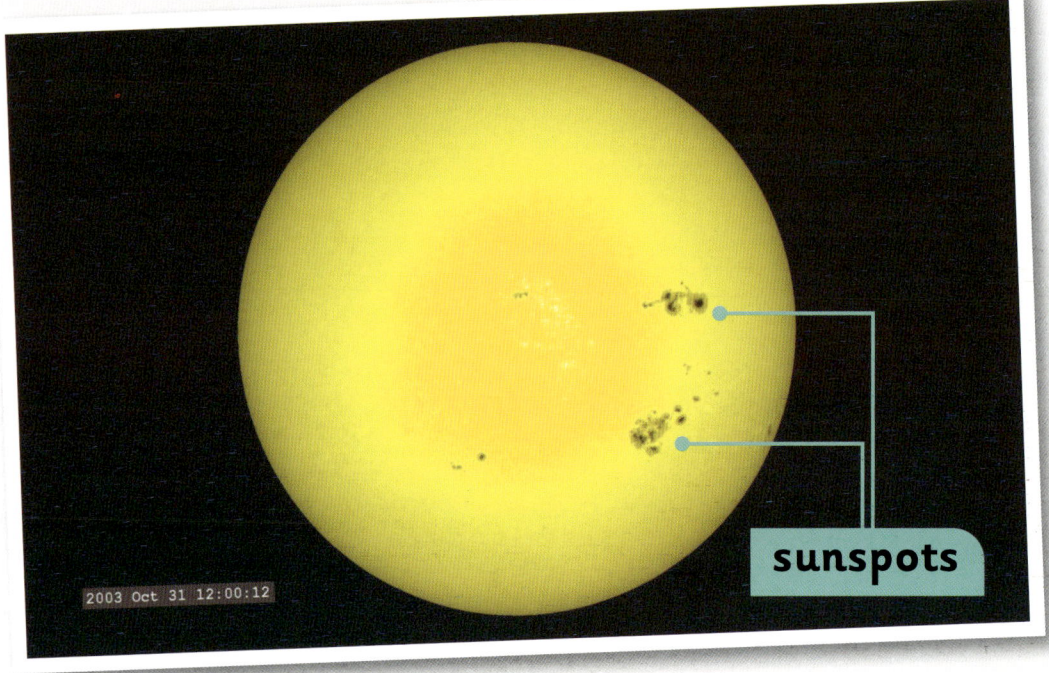

You can see some sunspots here. Sunspots can be there for a few days or weeks.

Sometimes, the Moon comes between the Sun and the Earth, and blocks out all of the sunlight. This is called an eclipse. When there is an eclipse, the sky goes dark.

You must never look at the Sun — even in an eclipse — because it will hurt your eyes.

However, you can safely view an eclipse with an eclipse viewer.

## How to make an eclipse viewer

1. Take a cardboard box.
2. Cut a sheet of white card so that it is the same size as the bottom of your box.
3. Stick the card to the bottom of the box on the inside. Then close the box.

**You will need:**
a box,
tape,
foil,
a pin,
white card,
scissors.

4. Make two holes at the top of the box.

5. Wrap one of the holes in foil and stick it down. The other hole is the one you look into.

6. Use a pin to make a small hole in the foil.

7. Remember to stand with your back to the Sun to view the eclipse.

4
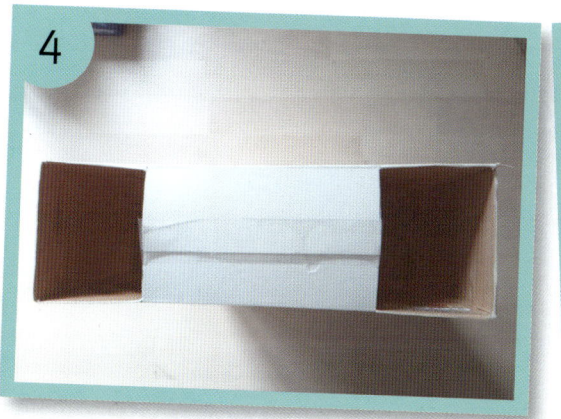

5
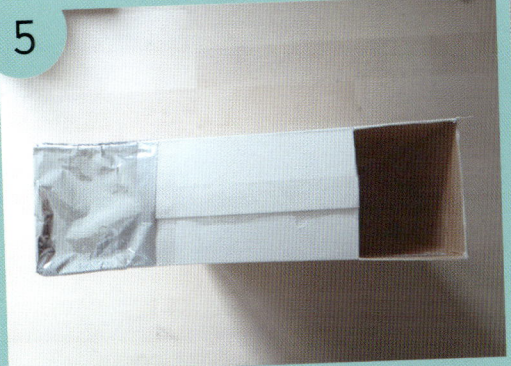

6
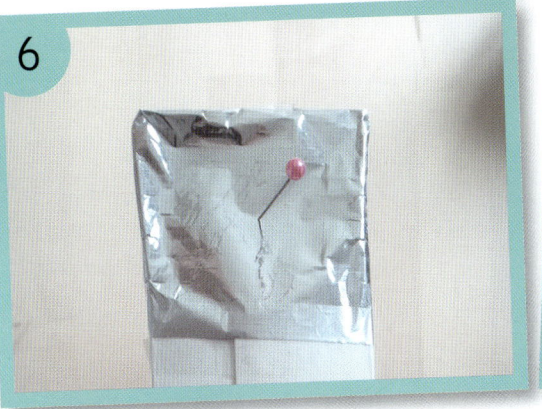

7

It is not just light and heat that make their way from the Sun to the Earth. Solar (/**Soa**lar/) winds from the Sun can reach Earth, too.

These winds make ribbons or curtains of green and pink light in the skies around the North and South Poles. We call these light shows the Northern (or Southern) Lights.

Norway and Sweden are good spots to see the Northern Lights.

Did you know that the Sun is the reason we have summer and winter? As the Earth travels around the Sun, it spins on its axis (a tilted line between the North and South poles).

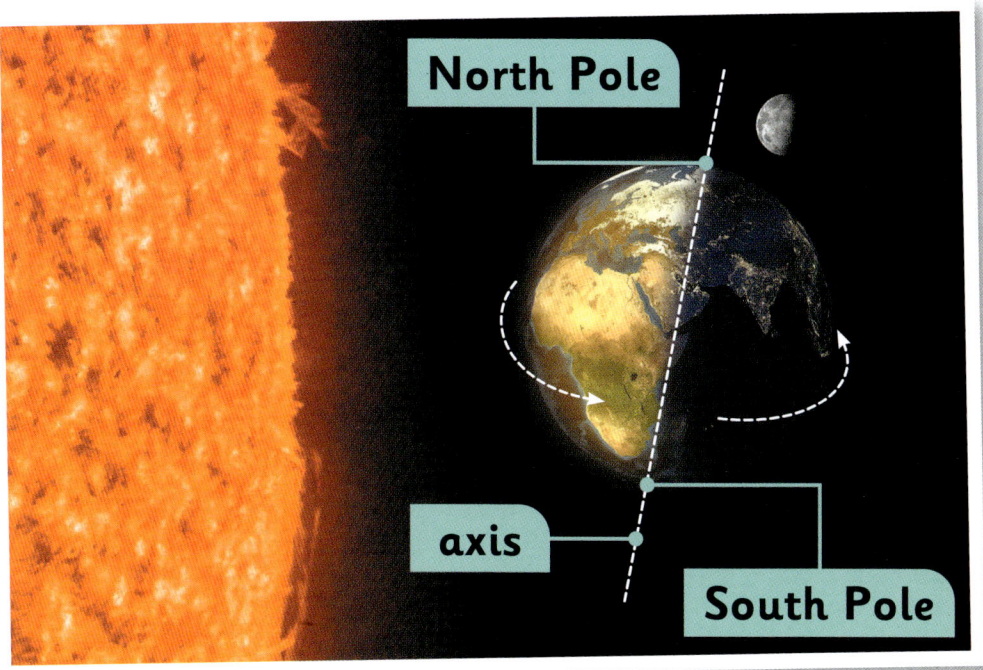

When the side of the planet we are on is tilted closer to the Sun, we can feel more of the Sun's heat and light. This is summer. When it is tilted away from the Sun, we feel less heat and light. This is winter.

Have you ever seen a building with black panels on the roof? These are called solar (/**soa**lar/) panels. They absorb sunlight and use it to power our electric lights, laptops, TVs and tablets.

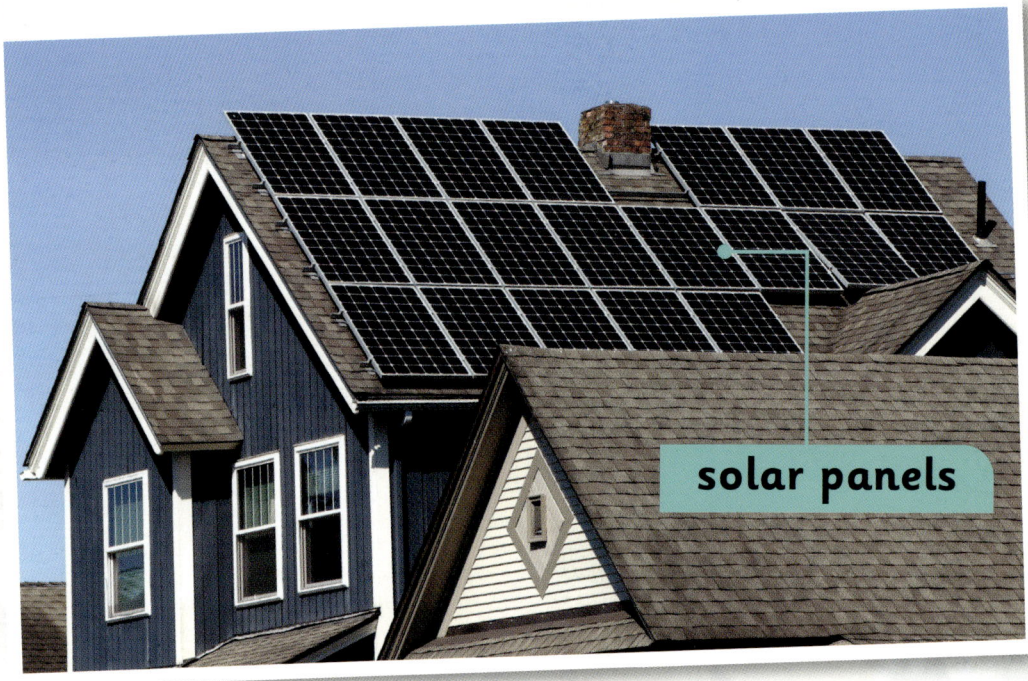

solar panels

Solar power is a form of renewable energy (/**en**erjee/). Renewable energy is made from things that cannot be used up, such as wind and sunlight. It is very good for the planet.